Take a trip to
BRAZIL

Keith Lye

General Editor

Henry Pluckrose

Franklin Watts

London   New York   Sydney   Toronto

Facts about Brazil

Area:
8,511,965 sq. km.
(3,286,668 sq. miles).
Brazil is the world's
fifth largest country.

Population:
119,099,000 (1980)

Capital:
Brasília (pop. 411,000)

Largest cities:
São Paulo (7,034,000);
Rio de Janeiro (5,093,000);
Salvador (1,496,000);
Belo Horizonte (1,442,000)

Official language:
Portuguese

Main religion:
Christianity (Roman
Catholic)

Major exports:
Coffee beans, machinery
and vehicles, soya beans,
cocoa beans

Currency:
Cruzeiro

Franklin Watts Limited
12a Golden Square
London W1

ISBN: UK Edition 0 86313 069 0
ISBN: US Edition 0 531 04736 9

© Franklin Watts Limited 1983

Typeset by Ace Filmsetting Ltd,
Frome, Somerset
Printed in Hong Kong

Text Editor: Brenda Williams
Maps: Tony Payne
Design: Mushroom Production
Stamps: Stanley Gibbons Limited
Photographs: Zefa; Colorpix/Ron Carter,
4, 12, 22, 25; J. Allan Cash, 14, 17, 24,
26; Marion and Tony Morrison, 31
Front and Back Covers: Zefa

Brazil is South America's largest
country. Through it runs the River
Amazon, the world's second longest
river, which is 6,437 km (4,000 miles)
long. The hot, wet Amazon basin is
crossed by the equator and covered
by the world's largest rain forests,
the selvas.

3

Manaus is the capital of the state of Amazonas. It is 1,600 km (994 miles) from the Atlantic Ocean. This major port stands on the River Negro, 19 km (12 miles) from the point where the Negro joins the Amazon. Ocean-going ships can reach Manaus.

Tiny Indian villages stand in forest clearings. The Indians of South America were the first people to live in Brazil. In 1500 there may have been two million Indians. Today there are about 200,000. Some still live by hunting.

The Amazon region is being developed as the forest is cut down. This means that changes are happening quickly for the Indians. Many lack resistance to common diseases brought from outside. Here a doctor flies in to give medical aid.

Brasília was specially built as a new capital city and was opened in 1960. Brazil is a republic, with a president as head of the federal government. The country has 22 states, each with its own government, 4 federal territories and 1 federal district.

This picture shows some Brazilian stamps and money. The main unit of currency is the cruzeiro, which is divided into 100 centavos.

WORLD MAP

Brazil

COLOMBIA
VENEZUELA
GUYANA
SURINAM
Fr. GUIANA
ATLANTIC OCEAN

Negro

Manaus
Amazon

Belém

Fortaleza

Madeira
Tapajos
Xingu
Tocantins
São Francisco

Recife

PERU

B R A Z I L

Salvador

Brazilian Highlands

PACIFIC OCEAN

BOLIVIA

Brasília

Belo Horizonte

Paraná

PARAGUAY

São Paulo

Rio de Janeiro

Curitiba

ARGENTINA

Pôrto Alegre

URUGUAY

9

The Portuguese arrived in Brazil in 1500 and ruled it until 1822. Because of this, streets in the old part of the city of Salvador look much like some streets in Portugal.

Three out of every four Brazilians
are descended from Europeans,
mostly Portuguese. But Brazil's arts
and traditions are very mixed. Here,
traditional crafts are sold in a São
Paulo square.

These young people pose for a photograph in a busy market in Salvador, the capital of Bahia state. Many Brazilians have a mixture of European, Indian and Black ancestors.

São Paulo is Brazil's largest city
and the greatest industrial city in
South America. It is also important
for banking and the arts.

Brazil's second largest city is Rio de Janeiro, and at night it is a blaze of lights. Its best known landmark is Sugar Loaf Mountain, which overlooks the city's port.

In Rio de Janeiro, like some other cities, there are slums called favelas. Many country people have flocked to the cities in search of jobs. There are not enough proper homes in the cities for these workers.

Coffee beans are dried in the sun at Campinas, 80 km (50 miles) north-west of São Paulo. Brazil is the world's leading producer of coffee. Coffee is the country's chief export.

The state of São Paulo is important for farming. It has fertile soils, a good climate and many modern farms. Three out of every ten Brazilians work on the land and the country produces nearly all the food it needs.

A Brazilian worker taps a rubber tree. This tree comes from Brazil, but is now grown in many other countries. Brazil no longer produces much rubber.

The state of Bahia in eastern
Brazil produces most of the country's
cocoa. Cocoa is made from the seeds
in the yellow pods of the cacao tree.
The seeds are called cocoa beans.

Sheep are herded by gauchos
(cowboys) on large ranches in the
southern state of Rio Grande do Sul.
Southern Brazil has a temperate
climate. Cattle, goats and pigs are
also raised there.

Many Indians in Brazil work at traditional industries, such as basket-weaving. Some Indians have followed European ways of life. Others live in remote areas and are only now meeting the outside world.

By law, children in Brazil must spend eight years at school. But in some remote areas there are no schools. One out of every four adults in Brazil cannot read or write.

Nine out of every ten Brazilians
are Roman Catholics. The church
plays an important part in everyday
life, education and medicine. The old
church of São Francisco Convent is
in Salvador. Its woodwork is hand-
carved and covered with gold.

This vast fruit and vegetable
market is in the city of São Paulo.
Brazilian food is very varied. It
includes dishes from African, Indian,
Portuguese and other European
cooking.

The sunny Copacabana beach in Rio de Janeiro is often crowded, especially at weekends. Most Brazilians who live near the sea enjoy meeting their friends on the beaches. They spend much of their spare time there.

Maracana Football Stadium is in Rio de Janeiro. Soccer is called futebol in Brazil and is by far the most popular sport. Brazil's national team has won the World Cup three times.

Rio de Janeiro's carnival takes place over five nights and four days before Lent. This famous festival is celebrated all over Brazil. All work comes to a stop for the carnival.

Brazil is rich in minerals, most of which have not yet been used. This iron mine is near Belo Horizonte in the state of Minas Gerais.

One out of every four Brazilians works in manufacturing industries. This picture shows a Volkswagen car assembly plant in São Paulo.

A new bridge links Rio de Janeiro to the industrial city of Niteroi, on the opposite shore of Guanabara Bay. Seven out of every ten Brazilians live in cities and towns.

The number of people living in Brazil is growing quickly, and Brazilians are mostly young and energetic. With its great store of natural wealth and use of technology, Brazil is fast becoming a modern industrialized country.

Index